Restore Us to Memory

a Sermon by

Rev. "Twinkle" Marie Manning

Matrika Press
a Sermon in My Pocket Series

Thoughts for Contemplation:

"In the quiet of the deepness
of the journey,
When the darkness is whole:
You are lovely;
You are comfort;
You're forever!
Because I have loved, I am changed;
Because I have loved, I can see.
Because I have loved, I am changed;
Because I am loved, I am free.
Where love has been, love will remain."

- Sheryl Crow

"Memory is not just a then,
recalled in a now,
the past is never just the past,
memory is a pulse
passing through all created life."

- David Whyte

Dedication

For my children & grandchildren;
For my friends;
For the congregations I serve.

I hold you forever in my memory.
You are cherished gifts to me
and you are a blessing to the world!

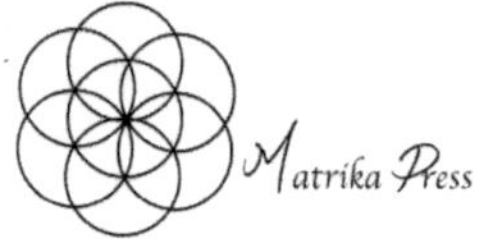
Matrika Press

ABOUT THIS BOOK SERIES

"a Sermon in My Pocket" series is
part of the "a Pocketful Book" collection
by Matrika Press.

This collection of pocket-sized books (4×6) are ideal
for poetry, meditations,
sermons or reflections, or
a collection of quotes and ideas.

This size is optimal for seasoned authors wishing to
offer a glimpse of their work
to readers in a pocket-size easy-to-carry edi-
tion. Also, this is an accessible first
endeavor for emerging authors
who desire to publish.

It is with delight we include in our
"a Sermon in My Pocket" series this
sermon by Rev. "Twinkle" Marie Manning entitled,
"Restore Us to Memory."

Her sermon was presented originally on
November 11th, 2018 to Starr King
Unitarian Universalist Fellowship
in Plymouth, NH, USA.
It has since become one of
Rev. "Twinkle" Marie Manning's
most popular messages.

Opening Words

Let us turn our attention to the sacred as we consider the words of Poet David Whyte when he says:

"Memory is not just a then,
recalled in a now,
the past is never just the past,
memory is a pulse passing through
all created life,
a wave form,
a then continually becoming other thens,
all the while creating a continual
but almost untouchable
now.

Every human life
holds the power
of this immense inherited pulse,
holds and then supercharges it,
according to the way
we inhabit our identities
in the untouchable now.

Memory is an invitation
to the source of our life,
to a fuller participation in the now,
to a future about to happen,
but ultimately to a frontier identity
that holds them all at once.
Memory makes the 'now' fully inhabitable."

Let us accept this invitation
and explore together this Gift of Memory.

Sermon:
Restore Us to Memory

by Rev. "Twinkle" Marie Manning

Mnemosyne (Nem-o-scene-y),
the Greek goddess of Memory,
was considered one of the
most powerful
goddesses of her time.

Revered during a time when
Memory was of
the utmost importance.

At a time long before
the written word
was incorporated into language,

Memory was critical to the
well-being
of an individual
and a society
who had to rely solely
on the lessons
and history passed on
in an oral tradition.

Mnemosyne is remembered
as being the mother
of the nine Muses,
each of which represents
what could be summed up
as the embodimental elements
of the human experience,
our expressions of:

History
Astronomy
Epic and Love Poetry
Tragedy
Comedy
Dance
Music, Songs
and
Religious Hymns

The memory of Mnemosyne
was all inclusive
— it was the memory of the rules
and energies of the universe,
the cycle of life,
the people, animals
and objects on Earth,

the memory of how
to live in the world.
And the world, beyond.

Mnemosyne's memory served as
protection, beacon, and blessing.

Another revered female figure
both Saint and Goddess,
depending on the source:
is Bhrigid, or Brigit, Brigid

also closely tied to the arts, poetry
and memory.

A prayer-poem dedicated to her
conveys how important memories
were to those of Celtic origins:

*Brigid of the Mantle,
encompass us;*

*Lady of the Lambs,
protect us;*

*Keeper of the Hearth,
kindle us;*

*Beneath your mantle,
gather us;*

And restore us to Memory.

Poetic examination of this text
indicates the use of "Mantle"
associates the theme with
the part of our brain
that plays a large role
in the processing of information,
in consciousness, awareness
...the creation of memory:
(the cerebral cortex).

We can conclude that
not only is this a beseeching
of being remembered by the Deity,
but also having one's own mind
transformed to a renewed
condition of health
so that the essence
of memory is whole.

This kind of desire
for memory and remembrance
is echoed through many
religious sources.

Many believe there is
an etheric Keeper
of such memories,
be it Mnemosyne,
or Brigid,
or St. Peter at the Gates of
the Christian Heaven.

At a human level,
We are each other's Keepers
– of Memories.
And, we want to share
our memories with others.

Along our journeys,
In our quiet moments;
In our public exchanges;
In our pursuit of
understanding the world
we reside in
and our purpose in it,
We are affected by each other.

And we want to be remembered
as who we know ourselves to be.
For being remembered
as who we know ourselves to be
means being understood.

To be understood creates
a sense of belonging
Which is an intrinsic
human desire,
indeed, an intrinsic human need.

Cultures around the world
for millennia
have left evidence
of their desire
to preserve Memory.

Pictographs and Petroglyphs
in Arizona;
Hieroglyphics in Egypt;
Cuneiform (Coo nā a-form) Script
throughout Iraq, Iran,
Syria, and Turkey

Each provide more than a mere

glimpse at primitive civilizations
that once existed;

Often thought of as the
mechanism to disseminate
the doctrines of gods
and dogma of humans,
these writings and pictures
also give insight
as to what once
were their daily lives,
family shapes and sizes,
rituals, cultural norms
and power structures.

The art portrays the observations
of these ancient people,
from documenting
celestial representations
of the solar cycle

to characterizing animals,
vegetation, landscapes
and waterways
of the natural,
and supernatural, worlds.

Some of such,
very subjective in its
observational tone,
drawing attention to that which
must have held significance
to the observer,
creating a better understanding
between ancient artist
and present-day patron.

One such example is of rock art
discovered a few years ago
in Egypt
depicting a herd of elephants

– one of the elephants
has a little elephant inside of it
representing a pregnant female.

Seemingly a small distinction,
yet at that point in history
apparently a rare way
of illustrating a gestating animal.

Carved between
4,000-3,500 B.C.E.,
this discovery in
the Spring of 2017
by an expedition of archeologists
led by Yale Professor
John Coleman Darnell,
was surprising to
the archeologists.

For while Ancient Egyptian
Hieroglyphics and art
have been widely found
throughout that region,
this discovery unveiled
monument size hieroglyphs
meant to be seen and read
from a great distance.

Compared to a modern-day
billboard,
the location of these inscriptions
show a kind of writing
that until recently
was believed to be only used
by the ruling class at that time
and used for
bureaucratic purposes.

Yet prominently placed
where they were
on what would have been
a route well-traveled by
the general public,
it indicates that the messages
on this "road sign"
or "wayside pulpit"
were readily accessible
to the understanding
of more than merely
the most privileged of the day.

In archaeological frameworks
what this means
is that the clock has
been turned back
and the point in time
they have long-believed

the Egyptian writing system
first became accessible
to the general population
is much longer ago.

And while we do not know
the artists and scribes by name,
their legacy,
their memory of their
time on Earth,
lives on,
grows and expands
though these findings.

Informing those who
have access to it.

Then and Now.

So it is, too,
with the memories
we are creating today.

Individually and Collectively.

Memory.

It is not just a recollection of
"What once happened"
Memory has a life of its own.

In the current moment.
Drawing on past,
present and anticipated future
to inform it.

The best way to preserve
Long Term
Perpetuation of Memory
is to pay attention to it
as it is unfolding,
the magical
and the mundane moments.

Scientists tell us memories
are encoded most strongly
when we are paying attention,
when we are alert,
when we are deeply engaged
and when information
is meaningful to us.

Protective measures can be
put in place
to better equip us
towards the preservation
of memory.

For we humans have some
obstacles to overcome
when it comes to what
we could call "memory thieves."

Mental and physical health
problems in particular
interfere with our ability
to pay attention
and to recall.

Depression. Isolation.

Also strip away our mind's ability
to hold with accuracy
recollection of past memories
and encoding of new ones
as those who are in depressed
and/or isolated states
are often focused on
past events
or
future worries
and replaying such over and over
in their minds.

And, as such,
they are not entirely present
for current moments.

Experts in the memory field
have noted that socialization
is another
contributing factor
to whether or not
our memories are strong.

Studies have shown
that people with high levels
of social integration
have a higher rates
of recollection.

It is suggested this is because
social interaction is akin to
mental aerobics,
maintaining muscle strength –
muscle memory if you will.

As such interactive,
uplifting conversations
are a good workout for our brains.

Stretching
– like learning a new
language or skill,
is like Yoga for our brains.

And while we are considering
movement and exercise,
as with the rest of our body
that improves its health.

With physical activity
that increases blood flow
including to the brain.

This along with
consuming nourishing foods
aide in the brain's Neuroplasticity,
which helps us to
organize information
and be flexible and welcoming
of new ideas.

And, today,
perhaps more than
ever in history...
Chronic Stress
is a key component
to memory loss.

Similar to Depression,
when we are in
Chronic Stress mode,
we are not fully present
for much of Life's
genuine experiences.

Chronic Stress keeps our bodies
on hyper-alert.

Many of us are overloaded
with work,
personal and family
responsibilities,
and the inundation
of negative media and news,
which are responded to
with increasingly urgent
calls to action.

One after the other after the other,
addressing multitude
of public concerns
that we focus on.

Our body's stress
response mechanisms
are meant to signal our minds
to become alert
and our bodies
to become activate.

This physiological stress-response
mobilization system
is designed to make sure
we can survive in a crisis.

And then reset.
Coming back to a calmer
state of Being.

Without extended calm periods,
our bodies become
flooded with chemicals
that result in

a loss of brain cells
and
an inability to form new ones.

This affects our ability
to retain information.

It affects our ability
to make good decisions.

It affects our quality of life,
and the quality of Living
we can engage with.

As a People of Faith:
We respond quickly to injustices.
We respond intuitively to the
needs of others.

With the rampant media
informing us daily,
even hourly,
of each impending crisis,
locally, globally.

With ever-emerging movements
tugging on our bodies,
minds and spirits
to contribute all that we are
in gestures of solidarity
so that we can make
the world new again,

Many are exhausted!

And, need to rest.

Now, I am not suggesting
you set down the
mantles of social justice,
for that would be *blasphemy*
if ever there were
such *sacrilege* to be named
in this creed-less faith tradition.

But what I am suggesting,
what I'm imploring
and what I am asking
is for you to
give yourself permission
to rest.

Instead of passing through
Life in a blur of
pressings and pressure:

Find balance.

Practice being attentive
to Nature,
to people,
to the changes of the season
and of the landscapes
and of the sky.

Notice the light
as it shines
through your window
each morning,

And the stars in the nighttime sky.

Notice each other!

Pause ... and notice how
your lover's eyes light up
when you enter a room...

Lover's.... *Let your eyes light up
when your lover
enters a room!*

Smile! Laugh!

Smiles and laughter
make memories.

So do tears.

Take time when they are called for.

Let them flow
and accept what
that moment offers.

Embrace this human experience.

Take a vacation
to explore something new...
Visit a sibling our cousin
or neighboring congregation
once in awhile.

There are plentifold ways
to access online these days
and at different times
during the week.

It is an opportunity to make
connections with those who share
similar values, hopes and dreams.

It is also an opportunity to connect
with those who hold
foreign beliefs,
philosophically, politically,
and a way to understand
more deeply
why they do.

Sing!
With many talented musicians
within your ranks,
I know I am truly
preaching to the choir!

So, Yes, sing!
And listen to music.

And Dance.
Move as you are able.

Dine together.
Hug each other.
Hold each other.
Rejoice in each other.

There is a Navajo Prayer
That says:

*When you were born
you cried,
and the world rejoiced.*

*Live your life so
that when you die,
the world cries
and you rejoice.*

Make memorable moments –
into memories.

Yes,
Healthy Diet and Exercise
Carefree Socialization
Loving Relationships
A Sense of Community
and Belonging
Mental and Emotional Rest
Spiritual Nourishment

All contribute to
better memory storage.

All contribute to
better Memory Making!

and

Restore You to Memory.

May Love reside here.

May you take time to rest.

And, may you live your Life
so that you rejoice!

AMEN

Closing Words

May the memories
you most cherish
continue to serve you;
And may you continue to make
good memories together,
and hold them close.

Remember you
Belong to Each Other.

Keep in Mind that
every moment is an opportunity
to make a memory.

Make ones
you want to remember,
And be remembered by.

May it be so.
Amen.

Navajo Prayer

*When you were born
you cried,
and the world rejoiced.*

*Live your life so
that when you die,
the world cries
and you rejoice.*

Discussing: Restore Us to Memory

Key Words and Phrases:

Mnemosyne
The Nine Muses
Memory
Keepers of Memories
Memory Thieves
Chronic Stress
Neuroplasticity
Belonging

Talking Points:

1. Who was Mnemosyne? And, what did The Nine Muses represent?

2. What other figures in history and/or mythology were known to be Keepers of Memories?

3.(a) How do pictographs, petroglyphs, hieroglyphics and cuneiform script found worldwide indicate the importance of memory to the human experience, especially preserving memory?

(b) What is significant about the rock art discovered in Egypt depicting a herd of elephants - specifically with one representing a pregnant female?

4. Individually and Collectively, how does Memory have a life of its own?

5. What are the best ways to preserve Long Term Perpetuation of Memory?

6. What in our modern society serves as "memory thieves" and how do they contribute to isolation and depression?

7. Regarding Neuroplasticity
(a) Why does a healthy social life contribute to a sense of belonging?
(b) Why is it important to be present in the moment with others?
(c) How do you personally find ways to engage in memory-preserving activities?
(d) How can congregations be proactive to encourage a sense of belonging within their members.

8. What are some of your favorite memories?

9. How do you want to be remembered?

Rev. Dr. "Twinkle" Marie Manning, D.D. is an ordained interfaith minister, retreat leader, poet and liturgist. She received her Doctor of Divinity, D.D. through the University of Sedona and is a member of the International Metaphysical Ministry. Twinkle strives to include many philosophies in her service. Her ministry often focuses on the earth-centered, esoteric, spiritually connected, community building and social justice aspects of her faith.

One of her ministry's core teachings is that of
Living Life As A Prayer.

Twinkle is a multi-disciplinary artist. She a published author and poet, intuitive acrylic and watercolor painter, mystical sketch-artist utilizing pencil, ink and charcoal, with additional creations spanning video, audio and digital media.

She is an award-winning television producer and podcast host. She is a former radio talk show host, columnist and luxury lifestyle magazine editor. She is an experienced public speaker, retreat leader and interfaith minister.

While most her published work is inspirational non-fiction and poetry, Twinkle has recently published her first children's book and is about to publish her first young adult and contemporary adult trade fiction novels.

Her poetry and writings
have been included in
spiritual rituals, funerals,
memorials, wedding
ceremonies, blessingways,
and coming-of-age gath-
erings in many locations
around the world.

Common themes of her ministry and writings
include:

Building The Beloved Community,

Curating Peace on Earth,

Embodying Compassion

Creating Spiritual Practices
that Honor the Earth and the Human Experience

For more information about Twinkle, visit:
www.TwinklesPlace.org

Matrika Press is an independent publishing house dedicated to publishing works in alignment with transformational religious and spiritual values and principles. Its fiscal sponsor is UU Women and Religion (www.uuwr.org) and Melusine's Haven (www.MelusinesHaven.org).

Matrika derives its name from the 50 letters of the Sanskrit alphabet called "the mothers" aka "Matrika." Kali Ma used the letters to form words, and from the words formed all things...as with the Bible: *"in the beginning was the Word."*

People of all backgrounds and faiths agree:
Words are powerful.
More than that: *Their vibrations are creative forces;*
they bring all things into being.

Matrika Press is part of the ministry of Rev. "Twinkle" Marie Manning and part of the larger nonprofit church known as Twinkle's Place, also known as RSOTDE. Matrika Press, along with TV for Your Soul, serve as the creative branch of the ministry's media projects. Matrika Press publishes anthologies, memoirs, poetry, prayer and ritual manuscripts, and other books to bring transformation to the world.

www.MatrikaPress.com

FIND OUT HOW
YOUR CONGREGATION OR GROUP CAN HOST
a local UU Talks in your community. UU Talks is a
speakers series, similar to TED Talks, where Speakers
will speak about topics aligned with UU Values.
Join Us!
www.UUTalks.org

Above pictured: Inaugural UU Talks event
at the UUA Boston, 2017
Peter Bowden, Matt Meyer, Lydia Edwards, Rev. Allison Palm,
Jim Tull, Anna Huckabee Tull, Regie Gibson, Marlon Carey,
Rev. Hank Pierce, Rev. "Twinkle" Marie Manning

OTHER TITLES BY THIS AUTHOR

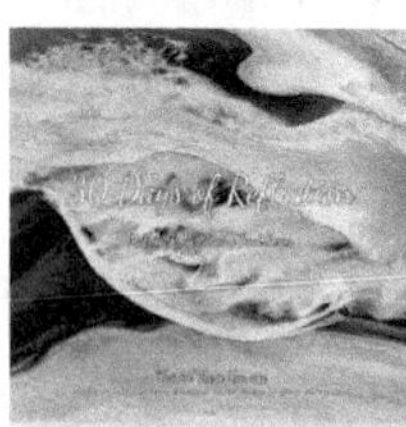

www.MatrikaPress.com

Cardinal Magic is the first book in the
Mora Mulberry series about a little girl who lives
by the ocean on a farm in Maine with her mother.
Mora and her friends are so happy to share their
adventures and lessons with you! This book is
about kindness and welcoming new friends. It also
offers strategies to help overcome stress.

www.MoraMulberry.com

GODDESS GUARDIAN
ORACLE CARDS

Designed by: "Twinkle" Marie Manning

Published by
MATRIKA PRESS

www.TwinklesPlace.org/GoddessCards

Empowering
W O M E N
Salon Gatherings
&
Signature Events

"Twinkle" Marie Manning
is the founder of the
Empowering Women TV project.
She and her friends host these amazing
gatherings! If you would like to attend,
or Host one,
in your community, visit:

www.EmpoweringWomenTV.org

Twinkle's Place

RETREAT CENTER & ARTIST RESIDENCY
www.TwinklesPlace.org

www.365DaysOfPoetry.com

PLEASE USE THIS SECTION TO RECORD SOME

OF YOUR FAVORITE MEMORIES AS WELL AS

HOW YOU WOULD LIKE PEOPLE

TO REMEMBER YOU!

Restore Us to Memory

a Sermon in My Pocket Series
by Matrika Press

This sermon by **Rev. "Twinkle" Marie Manning**
is about remembering (and reclaiming) who we are
and serves as encouragement to live our lives
in such a way that we will be remembered
as who we want to be remembered as.

It is also a call to create healthy lifestyles,
prevent isolation and depression,
cultivate Belonging
and be mindful about how we spend our Time.

9 781946 088345